Grammaropolis
PRESENTS

Meet the
Parts
of
Speech

8
POPULATION

Student Workbook
SECOND GRADE

written by
THE MAYOR OF GRAMMAROPOLIS

HOUSTON

Edited by Christopher Knight
Cover and Interior Design by Mckee Frazior
Character Design by Powerhouse Animation

ISBN: 9781644420317
Copyright © 2020 by Grammaropolis LLC
Illustrations copyright © 2020 by Grammaropolis LLC
All rights reserved.
Published by Grammaropolis
Distributed by Six Foot Press
Printed in the U.S.A.

Grammaropolis.com
SixFootPress.com

Table of Contents

Grammaropolis

Table of Contents

For information on how Grammaropolis correlates to state standards, please visit us online at edu.grammaropolis.com

FROM THE DESK OF THE MAYOR

There's a reason students can instantly recall everything that happened in their favorite movies but struggle to retain much of the important information you're trying to cover in school: people are hard-wired to remember what we connect with on an emotional level.

That's why grammar is so hard to teach. (As a former grammar teacher myself, I know firsthand.) Traditional materials are dry, abstract, and lifeless. There's nothing to connect with. Put simply, grammar is boring.

But it doesn't have to be! Our story-based approach combines traditional instruction with original narrative content, appealing to different learning styles and encouraging students to make a deeper connection with the elements of grammar.

In Grammaropolis, adverbs don't just modify verbs; adverbs are bossy! They tell the verbs **where** to go, **when** to leave, and **how** to get there. A pronoun doesn't just replace a noun; Roger the pronoun is a shady character who's always trying to trick Nelson the noun into giving up his spot.

And it works! Our mobile apps have already been downloaded over 2.5 million times, and thousands of schools and districts use our web-based site license. In other words, we don't skimp on the vegetables; we just make them taste good.

Thanks so much for visiting Grammaropolis. I hope you enjoy your stay!

– The Mayor

Meet the Parts of Speech!

Nouns

name a person, place, thing, or idea.

Verbs

express action or a state of being.

Adverbs

tell how, when, or where an action happens.

Adjectives

modify a noun or pronoun.

Prepositions

locate an object in time or space.

Pronouns

take the place of one or more nouns or pronouns.

Interjections

express strong or mild emotion.

Conjunctions

join words or word groups.

Grammaropolis

Meet the Parts of Speech, Grade 2 © 2020 by Grammaropolis

Meet the Nouns!

EXAMPLES

PERSON: <u>Melissa</u> said hello to her <u>teacher</u> at school.

PLACE: The family is visiting <u>Florida</u> in the summer.

THING: Daniel got a <u>bike</u> and new <u>toys</u> for his birthday.

IDEA: My mother offered me lots of her <u>wisdom</u>.

A Noun Names a Person

A noun
can name a person.

My **mother** always picks
me up from school.

Coach Smith teaches us how
to play soccer.

Let's practice!

Instructions:
Circle any noun that names a person in each of the following sentences.

EXAMPLE:

(Laura) ate ice cream after school on Thursday.

1. Robert likes to go to the park and play on the slide.

2. The teacher helped Michelle with her homework.

3. The police officer talked to all of the students at our school about safety.

4. That boy is good at playing the piano.

5. My father likes to play tennis with me.

Your turn!

Instructions:
Use the nouns below to write your very own sentences.
Don't forget to circle the nouns when you use them!

1. Clark _____

2. sister _____

3. librarian _____

Grammaropolis

A Noun Names a Place

A noun can name a place.

The trees in our neighborhood __park__ provide lots of shade.

Monica is learning about __Japan__ for a school project.

Let's practice!

Instructions:
Circle any noun that names a place in each of the following sentences.

EXAMPLE:

The three brothers went to the (theater) last night.

1. After dinner Lisa and Jennifer went to Lisa's favorite restaurant.

2. My family traveled to San Francisco and saw many sea lions.

3. Joshua went to Hunter's house after a long day at school.

4. For our class project we visited Peter's mom's office.

5. Nicole went camping in Alaska all summer.

Your turn!

Instructions:
Use the nouns below to write your very own sentences. Don't forget to circle the nouns when you use them!

1. Texas _____

2. beach _____

3. bathroom _____

A Noun Names a Thing

A noun is a word that names a thing you can perceive with one or more of your five senses.

FIVE SENSES

Vicky took **pictures** of the **animals** in her yard.

Let's practice!

Instructions:
Circle any noun that names a thing in each of the following sentences. (There may be more than one!)

EXAMPLE:

My (dog) likes to chase the (sticks) that I throw for him.

1. I won a gold medal for winning the race.

2. We use paint and brushes to create art.

3. Tommy organized all the pencils on his desk.

4. Alice used a broom to sweep all the dirt away.

5. My cat purrs whenever I scratch her behind the ears.

Your turn!

Instructions:
Use the nouns below to write your very own sentences. Don't forget to circle the nouns when you use them!

1. almond _____

2. telephone _____

3. octopus _____

A Noun Names an Idea

A noun can name an idea, which you can't perceive with one or more of your five senses.

Placing a **value** on **friendship** can lead to **happiness** and **success**.

FIVE SENSES

Pro Tip:
A noun that names an idea is called an **abstract noun**.

Let's practice!

Instructions:
Circle any noun that names an idea in each of the following sentences.

EXAMPLE:

Diana showed lots of (courage) when going through the haunted house.

1. Nancy seemed like she had no fear as she jumped off the high dive.

2. Yahtzee is a game that requires both luck and talent.

3. Sarah looked with disbelief at the beauty of the rainbow in front of her.

4. The kindergarten classroom was filled with chaos.

5. Lewis had always wanted to go on an adventure with his family.

Your turn!

Instructions:
Use the nouns below to write your very own sentences. Don't forget to circle the nouns when you use them!

1. bravery _____

2. envy _____

3. relaxation _____

Common Nouns & Proper Nouns

The **president** of the **country** has a lot of responsibilities.

George Washington was the first president of the **United States of America**.

Pro Tip:
*A noun that names a general person, place, thing, or idea is called a **common noun**.*

Pro Tip:
*A noun that names a specific person, place, thing, or idea is called a **proper noun**.*

Let's practice!

Instructions:
Circle any noun in each of the following sentences.
Tell if it is a proper noun or a common noun in the space provided.

EXAMPLE:
Have you seen what (Douglas) painted?

_____ proper noun _____

1. That man doesn't know what he is talking about.   _____

2. Mrs. Richardson sings so beautifully.   _____

3. I forgot to tell her about the neighbor's attack dog.   _____

4. They went to the same resort we did.   _____

5. She stayed at the Doubletree Hotel.   _____

Your turn!

Instructions:
Write a sentence that includes a proper noun, a sentence that includes a common noun, and a sentence that includes at least one of each. Don't forget to circle the nouns!

1. proper   _____

2. common   _____

3. one of each   _____

Meet the Parts of Speech, Grade 2 © 2020 by Grammaropolis   1

The **jaguar** ran through the **jungle** with incredible speed.

Jungles all over the world are home to wild **jaguars**.

Pro Tip:
*A **singular noun** names a single person, place, thing, or idea.*

Pro Tip:
*A **plural noun** names more than one person, place, thing, or idea.*

Let's Practice!

Instructions:
In each of the following sentences, circle any singular nouns and underline any plural nouns.

EXAMPLE:

Antelopes can run very fast over the grass and sand.

1. Orlando left his notecards at home, but he still gave his presentation.

2. After a long swim practice, Andrea ate a lot of apple slices.

3. Peter picks blueberries every summer with his sister.

4. Would you and Ruth mind sharing this table?

5. Camille uses stickers on her clothes so that they don't get lost.

Your turn!

Instructions:
Turn the following singular nouns into plural nouns!

elf	_____	mouse	_____
seashell	_____	door	_____
goose	_____	tomato	_____
loaf	_____	man	_____

Writing with Nouns

INSTRUCTIONS:
Brainstorm some of your favorite nouns for each of the following categories.

PERSON	PLACE	THING	IDEA
------	-----	-----	----
------	-----	-----	----
------	-----	-----	----

INSTRUCTIONS (PART TWO):
Now write sentences using some of the nouns you've selected. (Of course, now that you're a noun expert, you don't have to limit yourself to the nouns above.) Be sure to circle any of the nouns you use!

1. _____

2. _____

3. _____

4. _____

5. _____

6. _____

The Big Noun Quiz!

INSTRUCTIONS: Identify the noun in each of the sentences below from the available options.

1. Some computers can do millions of calculations in the blink of an eye.
   - ○ do
   - ○ Some
   - ○ millions
   - ○ can

2. Whenever Elbert and his sister fight, their father's anxiety level increases.
   - ○ his
   - ○ father's
   - ○ anxiety
   - ○ sister

3. Watching too much television has been proven to be bad for your health.
   - ○ much
   - ○ Watching
   - ○ proven
   - ○ health

4. Why should I give you this allowance when you haven't even done your chores?
   - ○ you
   - ○ this
   - ○ chores
   - ○ your

5. Vivian jumped in the pool before she checked to see how cold it was.
   - ○ jumped
   - ○ Vivian
   - ○ checked
   - ○ cold

INSTRUCTIONS: Is the <u>underlined noun</u> in each of the sentences below a common noun or proper noun?

6. When people tell me that my <u>city</u> is crowded, I have to agree with them.
   - ○ common noun
   - ○ proper noun

7. Can we go to <u>Dayton</u>, Ohio with my son, Dayton?
   - ○ common noun
   - ○ proper noun

8. Someone should definitely check that <u>dog</u> for fleas.
   - ○ common noun
   - ○ proper noun

9. I don't want to be alarmist, but has anyone seen <u>Mr. Johnson</u> lately?
   - ○ common noun
   - ○ proper noun

10. It's fascinating to see the different <u>ways</u> that various leaders act during a crisis.
    - ○ common noun
    - ○ proper noun

Grammaropolis

Meet the Verbs!

I am an action verb!

I express action.

EXAMPLES

Melinda **walked** to school.
Alice **kicks** the soccer ball.
Joseph **will do** his homework.

I am a linking verb.

I express a state of being.

EXAMPLES

Julia **was** cold outside.
That dog **seems** very happy.
Her pasta **will taste** good.

Action Verbs Express Physical Action

Louisa **smiled** while James **told** his joke, and then she **laughed** loudly at the punchline.

Pro Tip:
*When an action verb expresses physical action, it tells what a noun or pronoun **did**, **does**, or **will do**.*

Let's practice!

Instructions:
Circle all of the action verbs expressing physical action in each of the following sentences.

EXAMPLE:
Ellery picked the apple off the tree.

1. Mom locked the door to the house.

2. He swam in the ocean every day last summer.

3. Nikki cooked dinner for her family this week.

4. Everyone gave a standing ovation at the end of the play.

5. Sam and his father played in the back yard after school.

Your turn!

Instructions:
Write three sentences using action verbs of your own to express physical action. Don't forget to circle each of the action verbs you use!

1. _____

2. _____

3. _____

Action Verbs Express Mental Action

*Lauren **believed** in herself, and that's why she **succeeded**.*

Pro Tip:
When a verb expresses mental action, the action is not visible.

Let's practice!

Instructions:
Circle all of the action verbs expressing mental action in each of the following sentences.

EXAMPLE:
Eli (hopes) that one day he will be an astronaut.

1. He thought about the math problem all night.

2. Evelyn knows the name of everybody in her class.

3. Lionel depends on his older brother for help.

4. Amelia promised her mother a night without television.

5. Lucinda agrees with all of my ideas!

Your turn!

Instructions:
Write three sentences using action verbs of your own to express mental action. Don't forget to circle each of the action verbs you use!

1. _____

2. _____

3. _____

Action Verbs Express Action

Rebecca **baked** some cookies.

He **enjoys** the afternoons with his pets.

Pro Tip:
An action verb can express either **physical** action or **mental** action.

Let's practice!

Instructions:
Circle the action verb in each of the following sentences and indicate whether it is expressing physical or mental action.

EXAMPLE:

Mary's cat (plays) with my little brother's toys.   physical action

1. Jason packed his own lunch this morning.   _____

2. Her mother surprised her with a trip to Disney World.   _____

3. Lucas thought of his own recipe for clam chowder.   _____

4. Elena hopes for a spot on the volleyball team.   _____

5. The family ordered pizza for dinner.   _____

Your turn!

Instructions:
Write sentences using your own action verbs to express mental or physical action as indicated. Don't forget to circle the action verb you use!

1. physical   _____

2. mental   _____

3. physical   _____

Linking Verbs Express a State of Being

Linking verbs express a state of being. They "link" the subject to information that renames the subject.

"To be":
I **am** excited about swimming.
You **are** a good swimmer.

Pro Tip:
Linking verbs often take a form of the verb "**to be**" but they don't have to!

Not "to be":
You **look** happy today.
The flowers **smell** nice.

Let's practice!

Instructions:
Circle the linking verb in each of the following sentences.

EXAMPLE:
Lauren (was) exhausted after the soccer game.

1. Asher is remarkably strong for his age.

2. Alice became a musician right after college.

3. The fries at Bob's restaurant tasted awful.

4. Hazel seemed very happy this morning for some reason.

5. Something in Isabel's kitchen smells delicious.

Your turn!

Instructions:
Write three sentences using your own linking verbs. Make sure one of the sentences use a linking verb that is not a form of "to be." Don't forget to circle the linking verbs!

1. _____

2. _____

3. _____

Action Verb or Linking Verb?

Linking Verb:
The new restaurant's menu <u>looked</u> very good.

Action Verb:
When they <u>looked</u> at the new restaurant's menu, they were excited.

Pro Tip:
Some words can be action verbs or linking verbs depending on how they're used.

Let's practice!

Instructions:
Circle the verb in each of the following sentences and indicate whether it is an action verb or a linking verb.

EXAMPLE:

My shoes (looked) dirty after my muddy race.   linking verb

1. I felt so satisfied after my presentation.   _____

2. We felt around for the light switch in the dark room.   _____

3. My hamburger smells fresh and tasty!   _____

4. Her dog always smells the fire hydrants on our street.   _____

5. The instructions look too complicated for me!   _____

Your turn!

Instructions:
Write sentences using the verbs below as action verbs or linking verbs as indicated. Don't forget to circle the verb in the sentence!

1. sound (action) _____

2. sound (linking) _____

3. stay (action) _____

Verb Tenses

A **past tense** verb tells about an action or state of being that already happened in the past. (Most past tense verbs end in -ed)

Past Tense: Susan <u>knocked</u> on the door very urgently.

A **present tense** verb tells about an action or state of being in the present.

Present Tense: Susan <u>knocks</u> on my door every day after breakfast.

A **future tense** verb tells about an action or state of being that will happen in the future.

Future Tense: Susan <u>will knock</u> on my door tomorrow after lunch.

Let's practice!

Instructions:
Circle the verb in each of the following sentences and indicate whether it is in the present, past, or future tense.

EXAMPLE:
Eric (will watch) the entire play tomorrow.   __future tense__

1. Lydia rode her new bike all over the neighborhood.   _____

2. He will behave properly after the teacher's warning.   _____

3. Blake enjoyed the family vacation to New Mexico.   _____

4. Josey watches every dog-related movie possible.   _____

5. Mary invited her friends to the party.   _____

Your turn!

Instructions:
Write three different sentences using the same verb in the past tense, present tense, and future tense. Don't forget to circle the verb!

1. Past   _____

2. Present   _____

3. Future   _____

Irregular Past Tense Verbs

Amy **sang** loudly in the shower
I **lost** my pajamas, but then I **found** them.
Layla **took** a pencil home from school.

sing → sang
lose → lost
find → found
take → took

Pro Tip:
An irregular past tense verb is a past tense verb that is not formed by putting -d or -ed after the present tense verb.

Let's practice!

Instructions:
Circle the correct form of the past tense verb in parentheses.

EXAMPLE:

Eliza (shaked, (shook)) the dirt off the rug.

1. Kevin leaped out of his seat the moment the school bell (ringed, rang).

2. Tucker (hid, hided) his brother's pillow under the bed.

3. Last weekend, Summer (slept, sleeped) at her grandparents' house.

4. Hayden and Marcus (shutted, shut) the window so the rain wouldn't get in.

5. I immediately (throwed, threw) the spoiled milk into the trash can.

Your turn!

Instructions:
Write down the correct past tense verb form for each of the present tense verbs below.

give	_____	stick	_____	hear	_____
lose	_____	eat	_____	make	_____
spend	_____	leave	_____	teach	_____

Writing with Verbs

INSTRUCTIONS (PART ONE):
Brainstorm some of your favorite action verbs and linking verbs. Make different lists for action verbs that express physical action and action verbs that express mental action

PHYSICAL ACTION VERB	MENTAL ACTION VERB	LINKING VERB
-----------------------------	-----------------------------	-----------------------------
-----------------------------	-----------------------------	-----------------------------
-----------------------------	-----------------------------	-----------------------------
-----------------------------	-----------------------------	-----------------------------

INSTRUCTIONS (PART TWO):
Now choose TWO verbs from each of your categories and use them to write sentences in the spaces below. Don't forget to circle the verbs!

1. _____

2. _____

3. _____

4. _____

5. _____

6. _____

Grammaropolis

The Big Verb Quiz!

INSTRUCTIONS: Identify the verb in each of the sentences below from among the available options.

1. Whenever the person behind me claps his hands, I want to run away.
    ○ away   ○ claps   ○ behind   ○ his

2. Unfortunately, school is closed for the rest of the year.
    ○ for   ○ rest   ○ is   ○ of

3. Patricia feels really lonely these days because her cat is missing.
    ○ missing   ○ these   ○ feels   ○ because

4. Gloves protect your fingers when your fingers are at risk.
    ○ Gloves   ○ fingers   ○ when   ○ are

5. The grocery store is where people buy food.
    ○ store   ○ buy   ○ people   ○ where

INSTRUCTIONS: Indicate whether the <u>underlined verb</u> below is an action verb or a linking verb.

1. The theater was completely empty before the magician suddenly <u>appeared</u> onstage.
    ○ action verb   ○ linking verb

2. The magician <u>appeared</u> bored during what was supposed to be an exciting show.
    ○ action verb   ○ linking verb

3. Sometimes I just <u>smell</u> the roses even though I haven't stopped.
    ○ action verb   ○ linking verb

4. The back of my closet <u>smells</u> a bit funky.
    ○ action verb   ○ linking verb

5. Dayton's dad <u>grew</u> frustrated with Dayton's continued antics.
    ○ action verb   ○ linking verb

Meet the Adjectives!

EXAMPLES

WHAT KIND: My sister gave me a **_purple_** hat.

WHICH ONE: I always sit on the **_left_** side of the class.

HOW MANY: Neha invited **_ten_** people to her party.

HOW MUCH: May I have **_more_** ice cream, please?.

Using Adjectives to Describe

As George tiptoed through the <u>dark</u> hallway, he thought he heard a <u>loud</u> scream, but it turned out to be his <u>overactive</u> imagination.

Pro Tip:
*An adjective describes one or more nouns or pronouns. It can tell **what kind, which one, how many,** or **how much.***

Let's practice!

Instructions:
Circle all of the adjectives in each of the following sentences.

EXAMPLE:
The (old) (blue) car down the street still runs well.

1. Liam practiced on the beautiful piano for a long time.

2. The tall yellow birthday cake tasted delicious.

3. It didn't take long to figure out that the rotten smell was coming from the skunk.

4. Tabitha gave be a gorgeous bouquet of colorful flowers.

5. Elijah drank a cup of hot tea at the end of a long and cold day.

Your turn!

Instructions:
Write a sentence using adjectives to describe each of the nouns below. Don't forget to circle all the adjectives you use!

1. toy _____

2. squirrel _____

3. doughnut _____

Adjectives and the Five Senses

I walked into the **bright** sunlight.
That **green** mango tastes **bitter**.

Pro Tip:
*You can use your five senses
(taste, smell, touch, hear, see)
to describe nouns and
pronouns with adjectives.*

Let's practice!

Instructions:
Circle all of the adjectives in each of the following sentences.

EXAMPLE:
Harper just bought a pair of (yellow) pajamas.

1. A warm hat will keep you from getting sick.

2. There are only eight pigs living on the farm.

3. The classroom seemed too quiet for me.

4. Ryan wanted a sweet snack, but instead he got a stack of stale and mushy crackers.

5. The thick smoke made me cough.

Your turn!

Instructions:
Write sentences using your five senses to come up with adjectives to describe each of the nouns below. Don't forget to circle all the adjectives you use!

1. sweater _____

2. water _____

3. grass _____

How Many:
I have **ten** action figures in my collection.

How Much:
I bought **more** action figures for my collection.

Pro Tip:
An adjective can tell
how many (a number or quantity)
or **how much** (an amount).

Let's practice!

Instructions:
Circle the adjective in each of the following sentences and indicate whether it is telling "how many" or "how much".

EXAMPLE:

There seem to be twenty-seven icebergs in the picture.   how many

1.   Sara and Rudy exercised five times this week.   _____

2.   Some math problems are hard for me to solve.   _____

3.   Two halves make a whole!   _____

4.   We have fewer diseases now than we used to have.   _____

5.   Please give me more chocolate!   _____

Your turn!

Instructions:
Write a sentence using each of the words below as an adjective describing how many or how much. Don't forget to circle the adjectives!

1.   less   _____

2.   twenty   _____

3.   all   _____

Words Adjectives Modify

Adjectives before:

I swam in the __freezing__ lake.

Adjectives after:

Brian was __excited__ for the movie.

Pro Tip:
An adjective can come **before** or **after** the word or words it modifies.

Let's Practice!

Instructions:
Circle all of the adjectives in each of the following sentences. Then draw an arrow from each adjective to the word it modifies.

EXAMPLE:

Ella was (thrilled) when the (new) movie came out.

1. The chocolate cake was sugary and sweet.

2. The shy student was nervous to give a presentation in front of the class.

3. I find the sound of the beach to be soothing and relaxing.

4. In some old paintings, the grass looks yellow.

5. Jordan wanted more ketchup and extra fries.

Your turn!

Instructions:
Write sentences using the adjectives below to describe a noun or pronoun. Circle each adjective and draw an arrow to the word it modifies.

1. tiny _____

2. sad _____

3. white _____

Grammaropolis

Meet the Parts of Speech, Grade 2 © 2020 by Grammaropolis 3

More Words Adjectives Modify

Adjectives before:

The <u>purple</u> octopus had <u>eight</u> tentacles.

Adjectives after:

Hadley felt <u>exhausted</u> after the game.

Pro Tip:
An adjective can come **before** or **after** the word or words it modifies.

Let's Practice!

Instructions:
Circle all of the adjectives in each of the following sentences.
Then draw an arrow from each adjective to the word it modifies.

EXAMPLE:
The old manager is going to retire to become a landscape painter.

1. The brown dog chases young sheep on the family farm.

2. Ten silver fish darted quickly through the murky water.

3. Richard got a lovely new couch.

4. Mary enjoyed the gentle breeze on her morning walk.

5. Juliet brushes her thick hair with a special brush.

Your turn!

Instructions:
Write sentences using the adjectives below to describe a noun or pronoun. Circle each adjective and draw an arrow to the word it modifies.

1. quiet _____

2. crooked _____

3. hot _____

Using the Five Senses

INSTRUCTIONS:
Write down a list of adjectives you might use to describe things using each of your five senses.

SEE

shiny

....

....

HEAR

booming

....

....

SMELL

sweet

....

....

TASTE

bitter

....

....

TOUCH

hard

....

....

Writing with Adjectives

INSTRUCTIONS (PART ONE):
Brainstorm a list of adjectives you might use to describe each of the nouns below.

1. pencil	2. meal	3. tree	4. animal
-------------------	-------------------	-------------------	-------------------
-------------------	-------------------	-------------------	-------------------
-------------------	-------------------	-------------------	-------------------
-------------------	-------------------	-------------------	-------------------
-------------------	-------------------	-------------------	-------------------

INSTRUCTIONS (PART TWO):
Write sentences describing each of the nouns above using adjectives from your list. Circle the adjectives!

1. _____

2. _____

3. _____

4. _____

The Big Adjective Quiz!

INSTRUCTIONS: Identify the adjective in each of the sentences below from among the available options.

1. Henry is always excited to read books by Jonathan J. Jonathan.
   - ○ excited
   - ○ books
   - ○ Henry
   - ○ always

2. We're looking for some new volunteers.
   - ○ volunteers
   - ○ new
   - ○ We're
   - ○ looking

3. My friends broke into the dusty attic even though they weren't supposed to.
   - ○ attic
   - ○ friends
   - ○ dusty
   - ○ they

4. Some parents like to listen to loud music.
   - ○ parents
   - ○ like
   - ○ loud
   - ○ music

5. Nikki owns a guitar that is one of the oldest instruments in the neighborhood.
   - ○ owns
   - ○ neighborhood
   - ○ that
   - ○ oldest

INSTRUCTIONS: Identify the word the <u>underlined adjective</u> modifies from among the available options.

6. A <u>tiny</u> crack in the bathtub caused the water to leak onto the floor.
   - ○ water
   - ○ bathtub
   - ○ crack
   - ○ floor

7. I can't believe how incredibly <u>huge</u> the Grand Canyon actually is.
   - ○ actually
   - ○ incredibly
   - ○ believe
   - ○ Grand Canyon

8. Can someone please tell Joshunda where to find the <u>free</u> food?
   - ○ food
   - ○ someone
   - ○ where
   - ○ Joshunda

9. Lemons can be pretty <u>cheap</u> if you get them in September.
   - ○ them
   - ○ Lemons
   - ○ September
   - ○ pretty

10. Nobody has ever seen a platypus as <u>smart</u> as yours.
    - ○ ever
    - ○ platypus
    - ○ Nobody
    - ○ yours

Grammaropolis

Meet the Adverbs!

I am an adverb!

I can tell how, when, or where an action happens.

I usually end in -ly, but I don't have to.

EXAMPLES

TELLING HOW: Please run **quickly** to the store.

TELLING WHERE: I don't want to go **there**.

TELLING WHEN: The paper is due **today**?

Grammaropolis

Adverbs Can Tell "How"

Please look _closely_ at the picture on my desk.

When Susan tripped, she fell _hard_ to the ground.

Pro Tip:
An adverb can tell **how** an action happens.

Let's practice!

Instructions:
Circle all of the adverbs in each of the following sentences.

EXAMPLE:

Devin will (happily) finish the rest of your chocolate cake.

1. Victor studied hurriedly for the test yesterday.

2. I would like you to chew your food slowly.

3. Jaxon wrote the letter deliberately so that he didn't make any mistakes.

4. We walked home sadly when we found out that the doughnut store was closed.

5. I angrily snatched the stolen book from my cousin's hands.

Your turn!

Instructions:
Write sentences using the adverbs below to tell "how" an action happens.
Don't forget to circle the adverbs!

1. evenly _____

2. high _____

3. carefully _____

Adverbs Can Tell "Where" or "When"

When:
Eli had his first day of high school <u>yesterday</u>.

Where:
Stay <u>there</u>!

Pro Tip:
*An adverb can tell **where** or **when** an action happens.*

Let's practice!

Instructions:
Circle the adverb in each of the following sentences and indicate whether it is telling "where" or "when" an action happens.

EXAMPLE:

I will hand in my homework (soon.)

_____ when _____

1. I ran home after school ended. _____

2. I thought Kyla had decided to celebrate her birthday here. _____

3. Juliet searched everywhere for her lost kitten. _____

4. Please give me an answer now! _____

5. When the lightning hit, we all hurried inside. _____

Your turn!

Instructions:
Write sentences using the adverbs below to tell "where" or "when" an action happens. Don't forget to circle the adverbs!

1. there _____

2. tomorrow _____

3. later _____

Grammaropolis

Words Adverbs Modify

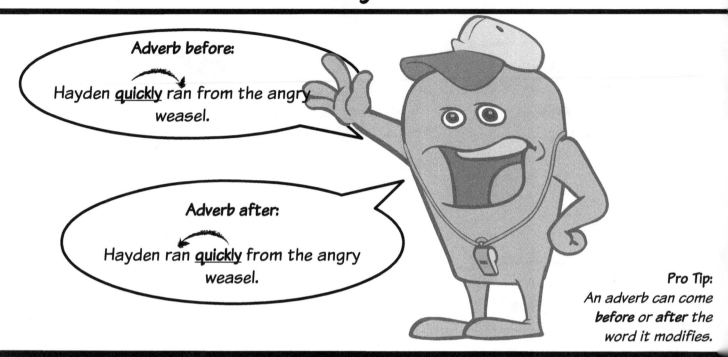

Adverb before:

Hayden **quickly** ran from the angry weasel.

Adverb after:

Hayden ran **quickly** from the angry weasel.

Pro Tip:
An adverb can come **before** or **after** the word it modifies.

Let's practice!

Instructions:
Circle all of the adverbs in each of the following sentences.
Then draw an arrow from each adverb to the word it modifies.

EXAMPLE:

Listen (closely) because I (never) repeat myself.

1. I always cuddle with my stuffed animals.

2. Beatrice hugged her mother affectionately before she left for school.

3. Henry strolled aimlessly down the street.

4. I sometimes feel as though my knuckles pop loudly.

5. Oh, they went there for breakfast yesterday.

Your turn!

Instructions:
Write sentences using the adverbs below to describe a verb. Circle each adverb and draw an arrow to the word it modifies.

1. lovingly _____

2. heavily _____

3. never _____

Identifying Adverbs

Modifying Verbs:
Kyle walked **quickly**.

"quickly" modifies the verb "walked" and tells how.

Modifying Adjectives:
Susie was **not** sad when I left.

"not" modifies the adjective "sad" and tells to what extent (how much).

Modifying Other Adverbs:
I wrote **very** messily.

"very" modifies the adverb "messily" and tells to what extent (how much).

Pro Tip:
An **adverb** modifies a verb, adjective, or other adverb. It can tell more nouns or pronouns. It can tell **how, when, where** or **to what extent (how much)**.

Let's Practice!

Instructions:
Circle all of the adverbs in the following sentences.

EXAMPLE:
My dog jumped (extremely) (high) and (accidentally) knocked my plate onto the ground.

1. The little girl down the street always gives me a very tight hug before school.

2. Gavin never comes here to play with me.

3. That joke is obviously not funny, okay?

4. I want to make sure that you always tighten your seatbelt securely.

5. To be completely honest with you, I am not happy at all.

Your turn!

Instructions:
Write sentences of your own using adverbs to modify verbs, adjectives, or other adverbs. Don't forget to circle the adverbs you use!

1. _____

2. _____

3. _____

Writing with Adverbs

INSTRUCTIONS (PART ONE):
Turn the following adjectives into adverbs by adding -ly to the end.

ADJECTIVE	ADVERB
1. _____quick_____	1. _____
2. _____sweet_____	2. _____
3. _____quiet_____	3. _____
4. _____grateful_____	4. _____
5. _____careful_____	5. _____

INSTRUCTIONS (PART TWO):
Now write a sentence for each of your new adverbs. Remember to circle the adverb in the sentence and draw an arrow to the word it modifies.

1. _____

2. _____

3. _____

4. _____

5. _____

Grammaropolis

The Big Adverb Quiz!

INSTRUCTIONS: Identify the adverb in each of the sentences below from the available options.

1. Pedro always remembers to call his mother after class.
   - ○ always
   - ○ remembers
   - ○ after
   - ○ call

2. The ocean water momentarily cooled my face.
   - ○ ocean
   - ○ momentarily
   - ○ cooled
   - ○ water

3. Someone should definitely look at the leak in our kitchen.
   - ○ should
   - ○ look
   - ○ definitely
   - ○ leak

4. Wilhelm stared intently at his brother until his brother noticed him.
   - ○ noticed
   - ○ until
   - ○ stared
   - ○ intently

5. My friend walked alone along the deserted beach.
   - ○ alone
   - ○ walked
   - ○ beach
   - ○ along

INSTRUCTIONS: Choose which of the available options is the word that the <u>underlined adverb</u> modifies.

6. Nobody <u>truly</u> understands how hard it was to grow up in my hometown.
   - ○ understands
   - ○ grow
   - ○ hard
   - ○ how

7. I <u>often</u> wonder what life is going to be like on Mars.
   - ○ what
   - ○ like
   - ○ going
   - ○ wonder

8. Mayor Turner made a <u>very</u> surprising announcement as the county fair concluded.
   - ○ surprising
   - ○ made
   - ○ concluded
   - ○ announcement

9. The point of the story is <u>not</u> that we are immortal.
   - ○ point
   - ○ are
   - ○ immortal
   - ○ is

10. It <u>finally</u> became apparent that Lucas had been right all along.
    - ○ apparent
    - ○ became
    - ○ right
    - ○ been

Grammaropolis

Meet the Pronouns!

I am a pronoun!

I take the place of one or more nouns or pronouns.

EXAMPLES

WITHOUT PRONOUNS: <u>Patricia and her sister</u> bought <u>the cake</u> for <u>my mother and me.</u>

WITH PRONOUNS: <u>They</u> bought <u>it</u> for <u>us</u>.

Why We Use Pronouns

Without Pronouns:
Jolene likes running, so <u>Jolene</u> is entering a race. <u>Jolene</u> hopes that <u>Jolene</u> will win the <u>race</u>!

With Pronouns:
Jolene likes running, so <u>she</u> is entering a race. <u>She</u> hopes that <u>she</u> will win <u>it</u>!

Pro Tip:
We use pronouns so that nouns or other pronouns in the sentence don't have to be repeated.

Let's practice!

Instructions:
Fill in the blanks in the sentences below using the pronouns from the word bank that make sense.

PRONOUN BANK:	it they her him them she we

EXAMPLE:

Whenever my brother yells, __he__ makes me anxious.

1. Patricia and Josephine are coming over tonight. Let's bake _____ a cake!

2. I checked a book out from the library and read _____ in one sitting.

3. Larry stole my idea for the project. I need to talk to _____ about _____ .

4. Kids can be really hard to live with. _____ always want to watch television.

5. You and I like movies, so _____ should watch one together.

Your turn!

Instructions:
Write a short sentence using no pronouns. Then write the same sentence replacing the nouns with pronouns. Don't forget to circle the pronouns!

_____

_____

Personal Pronouns

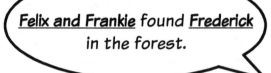

Felix and Frankie found Frederick in the forest.

They found him in the forest.

Pro Tip:
A personal pronoun takes the place of a person (and sometimes an animal or thing!).

Let's practice!

Instructions:
Circle the personal pronouns in the sentences below.

> **PERSONAL PRONOUNS:** I   me   you   we   us   he   him   it   she   her   they   them

EXAMPLE:
People always ask (you) to give (them) a break.

1. My dogs are tired. Do you know what is wrong with them?

2. He has never once given us enough water to drink.

3. She said you were going to were going to ask her a question.

4. That frog is cute, but we shouldn't kiss it on the nose.

5. John invited me for dinner. Do you want to come with us?

Your turn!

Instructions:
Write two sentences using personal pronouns. Don't forget to circle them!

_____

_____

Subjective and Objective Pronouns

Subjective:
<u>She</u> hates cilantro.
<u>We</u> never ordered that.
<u>They</u> always win card games.

Objective:
Don't give <u>her</u> any cilantro.
Why are you giving that to <u>us</u>?
We finally beat <u>them</u>!

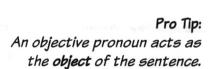

Pro Tip:
A subjective pronoun acts as the **subject** of the sentence.

Pro Tip:
An objective pronoun acts as the **object** of the sentence.

Let's Practice!

Instructions:
Circle the pronoun in each of the sentences below and indicate whether it is a subjective or objective pronoun.

EXAMPLE:

Gregory told his mother that green beans aren't good for (him.)   ___objective___

1.   It is always a good idea to wash your hands carefully.   _____

2.   Do you think vegetables are an important source of vitamins?   _____

3.   Don't give them any more chocolate milk.   _____

4.   I think most people would enjoy this novel.   _____

5.   This is the only time Pedro has emerged victorious.   _____

Your turn!

Instructions:
Write sentences using the pronouns below. Circle the pronouns when you use them and write S for subjective and O for objective above the circles.

1. me _____

2. I _____

3. us _____

4. you _____

Pronouns and Antecedents

Scott is making pancakes, and **he** offered to share **them**!

Pro Tip:
The word (or words) that the pronoun replaces is called the antecedent.

Let's practice!

Instructions:
Circle the pronoun in each of the following sentences and draw an arrow to the word it replaces.

EXAMPLE:

Diane is an amazing businesswoman. She really knows what's going on.

1. Carlton was so afraid that he yelped like a wild animal.

2. Aaron is hilarious. He always tells the best jokes.

3. My mother ordered me a blanket online, but she never gave it to me.

4. Lexie and David should be here any minute. What will they want to eat?

5. You and I are hungry. Someone should give us a box of chocolates.

Your turn!

Instructions:
Write sentences using the word pairs below as the pronoun and antecedent. Then circle the pronoun and draw an arrow to the antecedent.

1. Don/he _____

2. Giovanni/him _____

3. shoes/them _____

Writing with Pronouns

PRONOUNS: I me you we us he him it she her they them

INSTRUCTIONS (PART ONE):
Write a short paragraph without using any pronouns at all. You might want to use pronouns so that your writing doesn't seem awkward (especially toward the end of the paragraph), but control yourself! No pronouns!

_____

_____

_____

_____

INSTRUCTIONS (PART TWO):
Write the same short paragraph, but this time, replace ALL of the nouns in the paragraph with pronouns. This means that you will have an entire paragraph WITHOUT antecedents!

_____

_____

_____

_____

INSTRUCTIONS (PART THREE):
That second paragraph probably didn't make any sense at all because without antecedents, you couldn't figure out what the pronouns were replacing! Now rewrite the paragraph one more time using a nice mix of pronouns and antecedents to make your writing clear.

_____

_____

_____

_____

Grammaropolis

The Big Pronoun Quiz!

INSTRUCTIONS: Identify the pronoun in each of the sentences below from the available options.

1. I never know what to do with people who shave their eyebrows.
   - ○ people
   - ○ do
   - ○ with
   - ○ I

2. Whenever Jason gives us lemons, we make lemonade.
   - ○ Jason
   - ○ us
   - ○ make
   - ○ gives

3. Omar and his sister presented their mother with a poem they wrote.
   - ○ his
   - ○ their
   - ○ they
   - ○ mother

4. Talia told me that some animals don't like the water.
   - ○ animals
   - ○ Talia
   - ○ some
   - ○ me

5. Sarah said, "You had better come here right away!"
   - ○ Sarah
   - ○ You
   - ○ right
   - ○ here

INSTRUCTIONS: Identify the antecedent (the word the <u>underlined pronoun</u> replaces) from the options below.

6. "<u>I</u> don't think you should come anywhere near me," Jake said.
   - ○ Jake
   - ○ you
   - ○ me
   - ○ anywhere

7. Kyle, why don't <u>you</u> come over here and pick up the phone?
   - ○ you
   - ○ Kyle
   - ○ here
   - ○ phone

8. Bethany has a feeling that her dog only loves <u>her</u> because he likes walks.
   - ○ her
   - ○ dog
   - ○ Bethany
   - ○ feeling

9. This pizza is tremendous! You simply must have a piece of <u>it</u>.
   - ○ You
   - ○ This
   - ○ tremendous
   - ○ pizza

10. Rachelle said that <u>she</u> would give up eating cilantro for the next month.
    - ○ cilantro
    - ○ Rachelle
    - ○ give
    - ○ she

Grammaropolis

EXAMPLES

JOINING WORDS: Gavin's socks are usually yellow **or** green.

JOINING PHRASES: I generally brush my teeth in the morning **and** in the evening.

JOINING COMPLETE THOUGHTS: I did all my homework, **so** I get to watch television!

Coordinating Conjunctions

WORDS
Jake **and** Susan rode the roller coaster.

PHRASES
Do you want to wear this new blue shirt **or** that old yellow one?

COMPLETE THOUGHTS
The sun is shining, **yet** I just felt a raindrop.

Pro Tip:
*The FANBOYS (also known as coordinating conjunctions) are used to join **words**, **phrases**, or **complete thoughts**.*

Let's practice!

Instructions:
Circle all of the coordinating conjunctions in the sentences below.

EXAMPLE:
My dog had a lot of energy, (so) I took him for a walk.

1. Mario made a pie with apples, blueberries, and strawberries.

2. It looks like I'm having chocolate cake or vanilla cream pie for dessert.

3. I arrived early for the concert, but it was already crowded!

4. You and I like to read and write more than most people.

5. The schools are all closed, for there is a storm on the way.

Your turn!

Instructions:
Write sentences using the following conjunctions to join words or word groups. Don't forget to circle the conjunction in the sentence!

1. and _____

2. so _____

3. but _____

Conjunctions Can Join Complete Thoughts

Name:

We can use coordinating conjunctions to join two or more complete thoughts into a single sentence.

Without Conjunctions:
I got a bad math grade. I decided to study more diligently.

With Conjunctions:
*I got a bad math grade, **so** I decided to study more diligently.*

Pro Tip:
A complete thought (also known as an independent clause) makes sense all by itself.

Let's practice!

Instructions:
Join the complete thoughts below into single sentences using one of the FANBOYS. Notice that the meaning of your new sentence might change depending on your choice of coordinating conjunction!

EXAMPLE:
My keyboard broke, __so__ I need to take it to be repaired

1. The office is closed today, _____ people are working from home.

2. I don't know what you're talking about, _____ I promise to figure it out.

3. Don't worry about your pets this weekend, _____ Jay will feed them.

4. Vinny's car ran out of gas, _____ we had to walk the rest of the way.

5. The pizza is probably too hot, _____ I don't want to wait any longer.

Your turn!

Instructions:
Use the following FANBOYS to write sentences with two complete thoughts joined together as a single sentence.

1. and _____

2. for _____

3. but _____

Writing with Conjunctions

INSTRUCTIONS (PART ONE):

Make a list of your own simple sentences (complete thoughts that can stand on their own).

EXAMPLE:

The sun is shining brightly this morning.

1. _____

2. _____

3. _____

4. _____

5. _____

COORDINATING CONJUNCTIONS

for	and	nor	but	or	yet	so

INSTRUCTIONS (PART TWO):

Using coordinating conjunctions, add a second complete thought to each of your complete thoughts above. Don't forget to circle the coordinating conjunctions when you use them, and have fun!

EXAMPLE:

The sun is shining brightly this morning, (so) I need to remember to wear a hat.

1. _____

2. _____

3. _____

4. _____

5. _____

Grammaropolis

The Big Conjunction Quiz!

Name:

INSTRUCTIONS: Identify the conjunction in each of the sentences below from the available options.

1. I will always be here for you, for I am your family.
    - ○ be
    - ○ for
    - ○ family
    - ○ I

2. Texting, eating fries, and closing your eyes are discouraged while driving.
    - ○ fries
    - ○ closing
    - ○ are
    - ○ and

3. I am always fighting for truth and justice.
    - ○ justice
    - ○ for
    - ○ and
    - ○ am

4. My neck feels hot, yet the sun isn't even out.
    - ○ hot
    - ○ yet
    - ○ out
    - ○ the

5. Nobody knows my name, so I will have to introduce myself.
    - ○ knows
    - ○ Nobody
    - ○ so
    - ○ to

6. Kevin talked about letting me use his skateboard, but he never followed through.
    - ○ but
    - ○ me
    - ○ he
    - ○ followed

7. Do you plan to go to school or stay at home tomorrow?
    - ○ to
    - ○ at
    - ○ or
    - ○ home

8. Henry and his sister came over for a play date.
    - ○ for
    - ○ and
    - ○ sister
    - ○ his

9. I have no idea what you're talking about, but I like the sound of it.
    - ○ no
    - ○ about
    - ○ like
    - ○ but

10. Sometimes I want to give up, but I always figure out how to keep going.
    - ○ to
    - ○ up
    - ○ but
    - ○ how

Grammaropolis

Meet the Prepositions!

I am a preposition!

I show the relationship between the object (a noun or pronoun) and other words in the sentence.

I help tell where or when something happens.

EXAMPLES

WHERE: We're going <u>to</u> the store <u>in</u> the mall.

WHEN: Kyle walked my dog <u>in</u> the morning.

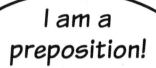

Prepositions Help Tell "Where" or "When"

When (time):
The mail will come **on** Friday.

Where (space):
Have you looked **under** the bed?

Pro Tip:
A preposition helps tell **when** or **where** something happens by locating an object in time or space.

Let's practice!

Instructions:
Circle the prepositions in the following sentences and then indicate whether each one helps tell when or where the action of the verb happens.

EXAMPLE:

Why don't you put your clothes (in) your closet?   _____where_____

1. I threw the ball over my neighbor's fence.   _____

2. Matthew will be spending the night on Saturday.   _____

3. I think you should look out the window.   _____

4. Garvin took me to the bank yesterday.   _____

5. Kelsey doesn't think she will be awake at midnight.   _____

Your turn!

Instructions:
Finish the sentences below by using your own prepositions to tell where or when the action happened. Don't forget to circle the prepositions!

1. <u>Kylie took a bath</u> _____

2. <u>Scotty and Huma ate pudding</u> _____

3. <u>Most people brush their teeth</u> _____

Prepositional Phrases

Pro Tip:
A prepositional phrase starts with a preposition and ends with the object of the preposition.

Let's practice!

Instructions:
In each of the following sentences, underline the entire prepositional phrase and circle the preposition.

EXAMPLE:

The game will be broadcast on television.

1. The biggest kid in my class is named Curtis.

2. Do you really think that there's a different world somewhere over the rainbow?

3. I leaned my bicycle against the wall when I got home.

4. Michaela had never traveled outside her home state.

5. We yelped at the same time.

Your turn!

Instructions:
Write sentences that incorporate the prepositional phrases below. Remember to underline the prepositional phrases and circle the prepositions.

1. around the room _____

2. in your mind _____

3. across the hall _____

Grammaropolis

Writing with Prepositions

INSTRUCTIONS (PART ONE):
Use prepositions from the Preposition Bank to create five prepositional phrases.

PREPOSITION BANK

above	behind	down	near	through
across	below	during	off	throughout
after	beneath	from	on	to
against	beside	in	out	toward
around	between	inside	outside	under
at	beyond	into	over	until
before	by		since	upon

1._____

2._____

3._____

4._____

5._____

INSTRUCTIONS (PART TWO):
Now write a sentence for each of your prepositional phrases. Don't forget to circle the prepositions!

1. _____

2. _____

. _____

_____

. _____

_____

The Big Preposition Quiz!

Name:

INSTRUCTIONS: Identify the preposition in each of the sentences below from among the available options.

1. Most people live within these twenty blocks.
   ○ within   ○ blocks   ○ live   ○ twenty

2. Alva gave a muffin to the little boy because he was sad.
   ○ muffin   ○ sad   ○ to   ○ boy

3. Many people from the United States speak more than one language.
   ○ United States   ○ from   ○ more   ○ language

4. Jacob knocked his shoulder against the cement wall.
   ○ shoulder   ○ the   ○ against   ○ wall

5. Please place the aluminum foil over any exposed food.
   ○ any   ○ foil   ○ food   ○ over

INSTRUCTIONS: Identify the object of the preposition in each of the <u>prepositional phrases underlined</u> below.

6. I promise that I will hand in my project <u>on Wednesday afternoon.</u>
   ○ afternoon   ○ Wednesday   ○ project   ○ hand

7. Have you ever been <u>in the middle</u> of a dark forest?
   ○ been   ○ forest   ○ middle   ○ dark

8. My rival stared at me, but I was glad that he was all the way <u>across the room</u>.
   ○ room   ○ me   ○ he   ○ across

9. If you look closely <u>at this picture</u>, you will find all the clues you need.
   ○ you   ○ this   ○ clues   ○ picture

10. I ended up with a big bruise <u>on my forehead</u>.
    ○ bruise   ○ on   ○ my   ○ forehead

Grammaropolis

Meet the Parts of Speech, Grade 2 © 2020 by Grammaropolis

Meet the Interjections!

EXAMPLES

MILD EMOTION: _Ouch_, that hurts a little bit.

STRONG EMOTION: _Ouch_! That really hurts!

Identifying Interjections

Mild Emotion:
Gee, sometimes I wonder what's really going on.

Strong Emotion:
Yeah! My team scored!

Pro Tip:
Mild emotion is set apart with a **comma**.
Strong emotion is set apart with an **exclamation mark**.

Let's practice!

Instructions:
Circle the interjection in each of the following sentences and indicate whether it is expressing mild or strong emotion.

EXAMPLE:

(Uh,) do you really think that's a good idea?   _mild_

1. "Argh!" she said. "I'm never going to get this right."   _____

2. Oh, I'm pretty sure you'll be home by noon.   _____

3. Hey! Can you please tell me when the money will be come?   _____

4. Man, I wish you hadn't said that.   _____

5. Eek! I just saw an enormous cockroach!   _____

Your turn!

Instructions:
Write sentences using the interjections below to express mild or strong emotion as indicated.

1. Shh (mild) _____

2. Oh (strong) _____

3. Ouch (strong) _____

Writing with Interjections

INSTRUCTIONS (PART ONE):

Write down ten interjections you might use to express mild or strong emotion. Feel free to make up a few of them if you want! Circle your six favorite ones.

1._____   6._____

2._____   7._____

3._____   8._____

4._____   9._____

5._____   10._____

INSTRUCTIONS (PART TWO):

Now write sentences using your favorite interjections. Remember to use a comma when you express mild emotion and an exclamation mark with strong emotion!

MILD EMOTION

1. _____

2. _____

3. _____

STRONG EMOTION:

• _____

• _____

• _____

Grammaropolis

The Big Interjection Quiz!

Name:

INSTRUCTIONS: Identify the interjection in each of the sentences below from among the available options.

1. Boy, I never saw that coming.
   - ○ saw
   - ○ I
   - ○ Boy
   - ○ that

2. Hey! Can someone give me directions to the stadium?
   - ○ Can
   - ○ Hey
   - ○ to
   - ○ me

3. Eesh, that was a close one.
   - ○ Eesh
   - ○ was
   - ○ one
   - ○ that

4. Um, I'm not exactly sure that you know what you're doing.
   - ○ not
   - ○ doing
   - ○ I'm
   - ○ Um

5. You really won the school competition? Hooray!
   - ○ You
   - ○ won
   - ○ Hooray
   - ○ really

INSTRUCTIONS: Indicate whether the <u>underlined interjections</u> below express mild emotion or strong emotion.

6. <u>Hey</u>, you're pretty smart to think of that.
   - ○ mild emotion
   - ○ strong emotion

7. <u>Yay</u>! I got a new job playing with cats!
   - ○ mild emotion
   - ○ strong emotion

8. <u>Ahh</u>, I'm going to have to get back to you on that.
   - ○ mild emotion
   - ○ strong emotion

9. <u>Wow</u>! This chocolate pudding is incredibly rich!
   - ○ mild emotion
   - ○ strong emotion

10. <u>Well</u>, I guess I can see your point.
    - ○ mild emotion
    - ○ strong emotion

The Big Quiz Answer Key!

The Big Noun Quiz!

1. millions
2. sister
3. health
4. chores
5. Vivian
6. common
7. proper
8. common
9. proper
10. common

The Big Pronoun Quiz!

1. I
2. us
3. they
4. me
5. You
6. Jake
7. Kyle
8. Bethany
9. pizza
10. Rachelle

The Big Verb Quiz!

1. claps
2. is
3. feels
4. are
5. buy
6. action
7. linking
8. action
9. linking
10. linking

The Big Conjunction Quiz!

1. for
2. and
3. and
4. yet
5. so
6. but
7. or
8. and
9. but
10. but

The Big Adjective Quiz!

1. excited
2. new
3. dusty
4. loud
5. oldest
6. crack
7. Grand Canyon
8. food
9. Lemons
10. platypus

The Big Preposition Quiz!

1. within
2. to
3. from
4. against
5. over
6. afternoon
7. middle
8. across
9. picture
10. forehead

The Big Adverb Quiz!

1. always
2. momentarily
3. definitely
4. intently
5. alone
6. understands
7. wonder
8. surprising
9. is
10. became

The Big Interjection Quiz!

1. Boy
2. Hey
3. Eesh
4. Um
5. Hooray
6. mild
7. strong
8. mild
9. strong
10. mild

GRAMMAR CURRICULUM CHECKLIST

☑ Innovative and engaging

☑ Aligned to state standards

☑ Addresses various learning styles

☑ Created and refined in the ultimate proving grounds: the classroom

THE STORYBOOKS

4/24/2019 | $6.99
Paperback | 32 pages | 8" x 8"
Full-color illustrations throughout
Includes instructional back matter
Ages 7 to 11 | Grades 1 to 5
JUVENILE NONFICTION /
LANGUAGE ARTS / GRAMMAR

9781644420157 | Noun
9781644420171 | Verb
9781644420133 | Adjective
9781644420102 | Adverb
9781644420164 | Pronoun
9781644420119 | Conjunction
9781644420140 | Preposition
9781644420126 | Interjection

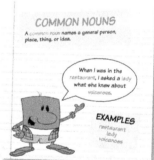

- An eight-book series starring the parts of speech, which are personified based on the roles they play in the sentence.

- Featuring a different character-based adventure for every part of speech.

- Each book includes standards–aligned definitions and examples, just like you'd find in a textbook (but way more fun).

THE WORKBOOKS

3/03/2020 | $12.99 | B&W
PB | 64 pages | 11"H x 8.5"W
Includes quizzes & instruction
Ages 7 to 11 | Grades 1 to 5
JUVENILE NONFICTION /
LANGUAGE ARTS / GRAMMAR

9781644420300 | Grade 1
9781644420317 | Grade 2
9781644420324 | Grade 3
9781644420331 | Grade 4
9781644420188 | Grade 5

- Skill-building workbooks featuring character-based instruction along with various comprehension checks and writing exercises.

- Aligned to Common Core and state standards for K–5.

Grammaropolis is available through Ingram Publisher Services.
Contact your IPS Sales Representative to order.
Call (866) 400-5351, Fax (800) 838-1149, ips@ingramcontent.com, or visit ipage.

Printed in the USA
CPSIA information can be obtained
at www.ICGtesting.com
JSHW060239160824
68134JS00058BA/2677

9 781644 42031